THE ULTIMATE TRAVEL JOURNAL ™

BEFORE, DURING & AFTER Your Trip

Graphic design by Bia Osmont Wahl, Portland, Oregon.

All photographs are originals from the collection of F. Michael Sisavic and are copyrighted materials.

Published by
The FLORIAN Group
Astoria Building
P.O. Box 1423
Lake Oswego, Oregon 97035

© 1987 The FLORIAN Group
All rights reserved
Printed in U.S.A.
Second printing 1989

Library of Congress Catalog Card Number: 87-81868

ISNB 0-9619093-0-7 Deluxe Hardcover Edition
ISNB 0-9619093-1-5 Hardcover Edition
ISNB 0-9619093-2-3 Softcover Edition

This Journal Belongs To:

_____

_____

_____

_____

WHY THIS BOOK
Was Written

 The ULTIMATE TRAVEL JOURNAL was written to help organize your trip and record the joys of traveling. It also provides you with a beautiful lasting memento of your experiences.

Traditional journals or diaries do not satisfy the needs of today's travelers. There are a few books which help in travel planning and plenty of travel diaries—but nothing like the ULTIMATE TRAVEL JOURNAL.

The ULTIMATE TRAVEL JOURNAL is a comprehensive travel companion which enables you to easily organize and plan your trip, record information needed during your trip, write an inspiring diary, and recall the best memories from your trip—all in your own handy personal book.

There are three sections in the ULTIMATE TRAVEL JOURNAL. Each is designed to minimize your writing time and maximize your enjoyment. The *BEFORE* section helps you plan your trip and record important information. The *DURING* section lets you write about your experiences as they occur during your trip. And the *AFTER* section enables you to summarize and recall the best parts of your trip.

With fill-in-the-blank ease, the ULTIMATE TRAVEL JOURNAL guides you through the planning details and develops the secure feeling of having control over all the important trip information. You will feel free to fully enjoy the trip—confident that the key information will always be at your fingertips. The easy-to-follow diary and journal section is designed to minimize the time taking notes and recording your experiences and memories. In the future you will be able to recall at a glance the best of your trip.

This book is a breakthrough which will make your trip more enjoyable and lasting. So, wherever your travels take you, use the ULTIMATE TRAVEL JOURNAL and have fun!

F. Michael and Irene A. Sisavic

CONTENTS

Why This Book Was Written 2

Personal Information 4

BEFORE YOUR TRIP—Getting Ready

Introduction		6
Budget Worksheet		7
Itinerary	◆ Master Plan	8-9
	◆ Transportation	10
	◆ Lodging	11
Before-you-leave Checklist		12
Postcards & Correspondence		13
Gifts & Souvenirs		14
Emergency Contacts		15
Packing List		16-17
Travelers Checks		18
Recommendations From Others		19-26

DURING YOUR TRIP—Experiencing

Introduction	28-29
Daily Journal	30-91
Automobile Use	92
Photo Log	93
New Friends Met	94-95
Currency Exchange	96

AFTER YOUR TRIP—Lasting Memories

Top Ten Memories	98
Expense Analysis	99
Next Time	100

Appendices

World Map	102-103
Conversions	104-107
Notes & More	108-124

PERSONAL *Information*

Name:

✉:

☎:

Passport Number:

Driver's License Number:

Auto Insurance Company:
☎:

MEDICAL & EMERGENCY *Information*

◆ Special Medical Condition:

Blood Type:

Eyeglass Prescription:

Other Prescriptions:

Physician's Name:
✉:
☎:

In Case of Emergency: Name:
✉:
☎:   Relationship:

BEFORE Your Trip

Getting Ready

Introduction	6
Budget Worksheet	7
Itinerary ◆ Master Plan	8-9
◆ Transportation	10
◆ Lodging	11
Before-You-Leave Checklist	12
Postcards & Correspondence	13
Gifts & Souvenirs	14
Emergency Contacts	15
Packing List	16-17
Travelers Checks	18
Recommendations From Others	19-26

INTRODUCTION
Before Your Trip

The BEFORE YOUR TRIP section of the ULTIMATE TRAVEL JOURNAL has many charts, forms and logs to help you plan your trip more effectively and with fill-in-the-blanks ease. This section also has plenty of space to record the variety of information you'll need during your travels.

Using the BUDGET WORKSHEET makes estimating the cost of your trip easy. All you need to do is fill in the form with your average per day and one time expense estimates and add them up.

Three ITINERARY blanks are included in this section to let you easily record your transportation, lodging and overall master plan. There is a CHECKLIST with important before-you-leave to-do items.

The pages for POSTCARDS & CORRESPONDENCE and GIFTS & SOUVENIRS provide handy places to list the names and addresses of friends and relatives you don't want to forget while you're away—don't forget yourself.

In case you run into some trouble during your travels, the EMERGENCY CONTACTS page has all the names and phone numbers you'll need. Listing the serial numbers of your TRAVELERS CHECKS could be important if you lost them. The PACKING LIST pages provide space for you to list all the items you take with you. Don't forget to add things as you buy them during your trip.

Planning for your trip can be great fun. Imagining where you'll be and making decisions is invigorating. A few travelers will be very organized knowing where they'll be and what they'll be doing every hour of every day. Others are less organized, deciding some of the details but leaving lots of free time for spur-of-the-moment activities.

The detailed planner will use every inch of every part of the BEFORE YOUR TRIP section while others will pick and choose. Read through each part—you might discover something you haven't thought about.

After your planning has ended, you can then carry the ULTIMATE TRAVEL JOURNAL with the secure feeling that the information you'll need for the trip is safely recorded and available at your finger tips in one private location.

BUDGET *Worksheet*

Per Day Expenses

		Estimate	
		Per Day	*Total Trip*
Food:	Breakfast	$	$
	Lunch	$	$
	Dinner	$	$
	Other	$	$
Lodging:		$	$
Entertainment:		$	$
Transportation:		$	$
Other: (Phone, etc.)		$	$
Per Day Totals:		$	$

One Time Expenses

Transportation:	$
Gifts and Souvenirs:	$
Other:	$
One Time Total:	$

Total Budget

One Time Expenses + Per Day Expenses:	$

ITINERARY
Master Plan

Date	Location	Things To Do

ITINERARY
Master Plan

Date	Location	Things To Do

ITINERARY
Transportation

Date	Travel		Time		Other Details
	From	To	Depart	Arrive	

ITINERARY
Lodging

Dates	Name & Phone	Address
	☏	✉
	☏	✉
	☏	✉
	☏	✉
	☏	✉
	☏	✉
	☏	✉
	☏	✉
	☏	✉
	☏	✉
	☏	✉
	☏	✉
	☏	✉

BEFORE-YOU-LEAVE
Checklist

- [ ] Decide location, time, duration and budget
- [ ] Get maps and guidebooks and make notes (see p. 19)
- [ ] Ask friends and relatives for recommendations (see p. 19)
- [ ] Develop and record itineraries (see pages 8 through 11)
- [ ] Make transportation reservations (see p. 10)
- [ ] Make lodging reservations (see p. 11)
- [ ] Check passport expiration date (see p. 4)
- [ ] Check visa requirements for foreign countries
- [ ] Check vaccination requirements and get shots
- [ ] Get medical and dental check up
- [ ] Check expiration date of credit cards and drivers license
- [ ] Get International Drivers License
- [ ] Pay bills due while away
- [ ] Arrange for a pet, child and parent sitter
- [ ] Arrange for a house or apartment sitter
- [ ] Install automatic light switches for home security
- [ ] Put valuables in safe deposit box
- [ ] Get money belt and voltage converter
- [ ] Have camera checked, buy film and new batteries
- [ ] Get requests for gifts and souvenirs (see p. 14)
- [ ] Arrange for gardening or mowing
- [ ] Tell the post office to "hold" or forward mail
- [ ] Get a copy of prescriptions including eyeglasses (see p. 4)
- [ ] Leave permission note for medical treatment of children
- [ ] Take sufficient quantity of prescription drugs
- [ ] Cancel or postpone newspapers and magazines
- [ ] Get travelers checks and record serial numbers (see p. 16)
- [ ] Get some foreign currency of each country
- [ ] Pick up transportation tickets
- [ ] Notify neighbors, apartment manager and police about trip
- [ ] Leave a key with family or neighbor
- [ ] Drain water pipes and cancel the garbage pick-up
- [ ] Turn off or change telephone answering machine
- [ ] Lower thermostat and clean out refrigerator
- [ ] Leave copies of itineraries with friends or relatives
- [ ] Complete the remaining forms in ULTIMATE TRAVEL JOURNAL

POSTCARDS & Correspondence

Name and Address	Date Sent	Name and Address	Date Sent
✉ Baldwin BOX 260 Earlham College Richmond, Indiana 47374		✉	
✉ Finch BOX 3434 CONN COLLEGE, NEW LONDON CT 06320		✉	
✉ T. Frank Comstock house Northampton MA 01063		✉	
✉ Iben 2417 Baja Cerro Circle S.D. CA 92109		✉	
✉ Wponlan 120 College Ave #207 Boulder CO 80302		✉	
✉ Mhunt BOX 2099 S.C.U SC CA 90095053		✉	
✉ H.Johnson Maynard Hall 800 FONT BLVD. 632B SF CA 94132		✉	
✉ Panda BOX 4854 Wesleyan Station 221 Highcrest Middletown CT 06457		✉	
✉ Wheary BOX 2748		✉	
✉ Steiner Leverett House Harvard College Cambridge, MA 02138		✉	
✉ Megan 4324 NE 41st AVE PTLD, OR 97211		✉	
✉ Panda # 203-638-1236 downstairs 203 638-4554 upstairs ✉ 203 638-0177 Brendan			

GIFTS
& Souvenirs

Name	Possibilities (Include Budget)	Actual Purchases	Cost

Totals: Budget = $_____ Actual = $_____
            (see p. 7)   (see p. 99)

EMERGENCY
Contacts

Travel Agent:
✉
☎

Bank:
✉
☎

Broker:
✉
☎

Credit Card Co.:
✉
☎

Credit Card Co.:
✉
☎

Physician:
✉
☎

Other:
✉
☎

Other:
✉
☎

PACKING List

Item	#	✓

Item	#	✓

Carry-on Bag Suggestions:

PACKING List

Item	#	✓

Item	#	✓

Other Notations:

TRAVELERS
Checks

Value	Serial Number	Date Cashed

Value	Serial Number	Date Cashed

RECOMMENDATIONS
From Others

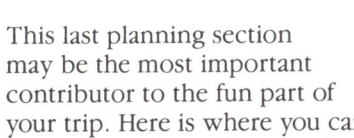

This last planning section may be the most important contributor to the fun part of your trip. Here is where you can record all of those "favorites" your friends and relatives say they enjoyed. You can also pick and choose from guidebooks and magazines and include ideas in this section.

Once you have decided on your destination ask everyone for recommendations—friends, relatives, travel agents, shop clerks and others. Pay particular attention to those unknown-to-guidebooks recommendations. As you read magazines, newspapers and guidebooks note those things you're attracted to such as restaurants, sites-to-be-seen and special events.

One last thing to include in this section—people to contact. Experienced travelers seek out people who live at the location they're visiting. These "locals" are usually happy to do some entertaining and certainly know the high-and-lowlights of the local area.

It's important to organize your favorite "favorites" by location—a city, country or hotel. This way, when you arrive there you can whip out your ULTIMATE TRAVEL JOURNAL RECOMMENDATIONS section and have the information you need for a great time.

RECOMMENDATIONS
From Others

LOCATION:

Where To Stay	Address & Phone	Comments
	✉ ☎	
	✉ ☎	
	✉ ☎	

Where To Eat	Address & Phone	Comments
	✉ ☎	
	✉ ☎	
	✉ ☎	

Must-See Sites	Events/Location/Dates

People to Contact	Other

RECOMMENDATIONS
From Others

LOCATION:

Where To Stay	*Address & Phone*	*Comments*
	✉ ☎	
	✉ ☎	
	✉ ☎	

Where To Eat	*Address & Phone*	*Comments*
	✉ ☎	
	✉ ☎	
	✉ ☎	

Must-See Sites	*Events/Location/Dates*

People to Contact	*Other*

RECOMMENDATIONS
From Others

LOCATION:

Where To Stay	Address & Phone	Comments
	✉ ☎	
	✉ ☎	
	✉ ☎	

Where To Eat	Address & Phone	Comments
	✉ ☎	
	✉ ☎	
	✉ ☎	

Must-See Sites	Events/Location/Dates

People to Contact	Other

RECOMMENDATIONS
From Others

LOCATION:

Where To Stay	Address & Phone	Comments
	✉ ☎	
	✉ ☎	
	✉ ☎	

Where To Eat	Address & Phone	Comments
	✉ ☎	
	✉ ☎	
	✉ ☎	

Must-See Sites	Events/Location/Dates

People to Contact	Other

RECOMMENDATIONS
From Others

LOCATION:

Where To Stay	Address & Phone	Comments
	✉ ☎	
	✉ ☎	
	✉ ☎	

Where To Eat	Address & Phone	Comments
	✉ ☎	
	✉ ☎	
	✉ ☎	

Must-See Sites	Events/Location/Dates

People to Contact	Other

RECOMMENDATIONS
From Others

LOCATION:

Where To Stay	Address & Phone	Comments
	✉	
	☎	
	✉	
	☎	
	✉	
	☎	

Where To Eat	Address & Phone	Comments
	✉	
	☎	
	✉	
	☎	
	✉	
	☎	

Must-See Sites	Events/Location/Dates

People to Contact	Other

RECOMMENDATIONS
From Others

LOCATION:

Where To Stay	Address & Phone	Comments
	✉ ☎	
	✉ ☎	
	✉ ☎	

Where To Eat	Address & Phone	Comments
	✉ ☎	
	✉ ☎	
	✉ ☎	

Must-See Sites	Events/Location/Dates

People to Contact	Other

DURING Your Trip

Experiencing

Introduction	28-29
Daily Journal	30-91
Automobile Use	92
Photo Log	93
New Friends Met	94-95
Currency Exchange	96

INTRODUCTION
During Your Trip

There are three goals in using a diary during your trip:

1. To more fully enjoy the experience by writing your thoughts and expressing your feelings on paper.

2. To have a record of your memories to be recalled and relived again in the future.

3. To ensure spending is under control and roughly in line with your budget.

This section of the ULTIMATE TRAVEL JOURNAL provides space and logs to meet each of these goals—plus some innovations to make your writing easier and recalling a snap!

Each unit of the DIARY consists of two parts geared for a single day's activities: a log to record expenses and other details plus a space to be used for your diary or journal.

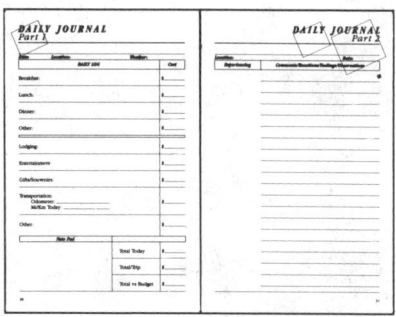

In addition to having space to record daily expenses, the first part can include anything you'd like to remember about the various activities. For example, in the MEAL section you can write about what or where you ate, who you ate with, the view, or any special feelings. With Part 1 completed, you have the information needed to estimate your total spending for the day, compare actual vs. planned expenses and make any desired changes.

INTRODUCTION
During Your Trip

The second part or DIARY section is like all other diaries with one exception—there is space to include a key word or heading for each EXPERIENCE. You can write a short phrase—for example, "Museum visit." Then you can describe each experience in as much detail as you'd like. If you need more writing space, use the NOTES section starting on page 108.

This method of journal writing triggers memories of the day and helps decide which things to write about. Scanning the EXPERIENCE column after your trip helps you find anything in the journal in a few seconds.

The DIARY section of the ULTIMATE TRAVEL JOURNAL can easily accommodate the more traditional diary—just describe things as you travel. Any way you do it, don't forget your first goal is to have a great time.

An experience becomes a memory instantly and if not written down, it may be forgotten forever. So try to find some time to write about your experiences—they're fleeting and worth sharing and remembering over and over. It's not difficult to do and with the help of the ULTIMATE TRAVEL JOURNAL, it shouldn't take more than a few minutes a day.

DAILY JOURNAL
Part 1

Date:	Location:	Weather:	
DAILY LOG			**Cost**
Breakfast:			$_____
Lunch:			$_____
Dinner:			$_____
Other:			$_____
Lodging:			$_____
Entertainment:			$_____
Gifts/Souvenirs:			$_____
Transportation: 　　Odometer: _____ 　　Mi/Km Today: _____			$_____
Other:			$_____

Note Pad		
	Total Today	$_____
	Total/Trip	$_____
	Total vs Budget	$_____

DAILY JOURNAL
Part 2

Location: **Date:**

Experiencing	Comments/Reactions/Feelings/Observations

DAILY JOURNAL
Part 1

Date:　　　　Location:　　　　　　　　Weather:

DAILY LOG	Cost
Breakfast:	$_____
Lunch:	$_____
Dinner:	$_____
Other:	$_____
Lodging:	$_____
Entertainment:	$_____
Gifts/Souvenirs:	$_____
Transportation: 　　Odometer: _____ 　　Mi/Km Today: _____	$_____
Other:	$_____

Note Pad		
	Total Today	$_____
	Total/Trip	$_____
	Total vs Budget	$_____

DAILY JOURNAL
Part 2

Location: **Date:**

Experiencing	Comments/Reactions/Feelings/Observations

DAILY JOURNAL
Part 1

Date: Location: Weather:

DAILY LOG	Cost
Breakfast:	$_____
Lunch:	$_____
Dinner:	$_____
Other:	$_____
Lodging:	$_____
Entertainment:	$_____
Gifts/Souvenirs:	$_____

Transportation:
    Odometer: _____
    Mi/Km Today: _____
	$_____

Other:	$_____

Note Pad		
	Total Today	$_____
	Total/Trip	$_____
	Total vs Budget	$_____

DAILY JOURNAL
Part 2

Location: **Date:**

Experiencing	Comments/Reactions/Feelings/Observations

DAILY JOURNAL
Part 1

Date:	Location:	Weather:	
DAILY LOG			**Cost**
Breakfast:			$_____
Lunch:			$_____
Dinner:			$_____
Other:			$_____
Lodging:			$_____
Entertainment:			$_____
Gifts/Souvenirs:			$_____
Transportation: Odometer: _____ Mi/Km Today: _____			$_____
Other:			$_____

Note Pad		
	Total Today	$_____
	Total/Trip	$_____
	Total vs Budget	$_____

DAILY JOURNAL
Part 2

Location: **Date:**

Experiencing	Comments/Reactions/Feelings/Observations

DAILY JOURNAL
Part 1

Date:	Location:	Weather:	
DAILY LOG			**Cost**
Breakfast:			$_____
Lunch:			$_____
Dinner:			$_____
Other:			$_____
Lodging:			$_____
Entertainment:			$_____
Gifts/Souvenirs:			$_____

Transportation:
    Odometer: _____
    Mi/Km Today: _____
			$_____

Other:			$_____

Note Pad		
	Total Today	$_____
	Total/Trip	$_____
	Total vs Budget	$_____

DAILY JOURNAL
Part 2

Location: **Date:**

Experiencing	Comments/Reactions/Feelings/Observations

DAILY JOURNAL
Part 1

Date: **Location:** **Weather:**

DAILY LOG	Cost
Breakfast:	$_____
Lunch:	$_____
Dinner:	$_____
Other:	$_____
Lodging:	$_____
Entertainment:	$_____
Gifts/Souvenirs:	$_____

Transportation:
    Odometer: _____
    Mi/Km Today: _____
	$_____

Other:	$_____

Note Pad		
	Total Today	$_____
	Total/Trip	$_____
	Total vs Budget	$_____

DAILY JOURNAL
Part 2

Location: **Date:**

Experiencing	Comments/Reactions/Feelings/Observations

DAILY JOURNAL
Part 1

Date: **Location:** **Weather:**

DAILY LOG	Cost
Breakfast:	$
Lunch:	$
Dinner:	$
Other:	$
Lodging:	$
Entertainment:	$
Gifts/Souvenirs:	$

Transportation:
    Odometer: _____
    Mi/Km Today: _____
	$

Other:	$

Note Pad		
	Total Today	$
	Total/Trip	$
	Total vs Budget	$

DAILY JOURNAL
Part 2

Location: **Date:**

Experiencing	Comments/Reactions/Feelings/Observations

DAILY JOURNAL
Part 1

Date:	Location:	Weather:	
DAILY LOG			**Cost**
Breakfast:			$_____
Lunch:			$_____
Dinner:			$_____
Other:			$_____
Lodging:			$_____
Entertainment:			$_____
Gifts/Souvenirs:			$_____

Transportation:
    Odometer: _____
    Mi/Km Today: _____
			$_____

Other:			$_____

Note Pad		
	Total Today	$_____
	Total/Trip	$_____
	Total vs Budget	$_____

DAILY JOURNAL
Part 2

Location: **Date:**

Experiencing	Comments/Reactions/Feelings/Observations

DAILY JOURNAL
Part 1

Date: **Location:** **Weather:**

DAILY LOG	Cost
Breakfast:	$_____
Lunch:	$_____
Dinner:	$_____
Other:	$_____
Lodging:	$_____
Entertainment:	$_____
Gifts/Souvenirs:	$_____
Transportation: 　　Odometer: _____ 　　Mi/Km Today: _____	$_____
Other:	$_____

Note Pad		
	Total Today	$_____
	Total/Trip	$_____
	Total vs Budget	$_____

DAILY JOURNAL
Part 2

Location: **Date:**

Experiencing	Comments/Reactions/Feelings/Observations

DAILY JOURNAL
Part 1

Date: **Location:**   **Weather:**

DAILY LOG	Cost
Breakfast:	$_____
Lunch:	$_____
Dinner:	$_____
Other:	$_____
Lodging:	$_____
Entertainment:	$_____
Gifts/Souvenirs:	$_____

Transportation:
   Odometer: _____
   Mi/Km Today: _____
	$_____

Other:	$_____

Note Pad		
	Total Today	$_____
	Total/Trip	$_____
	Total vs Budget	$_____

DAILY JOURNAL
Part 2

Location: **Date:**

Experiencing	Comments/Reactions/Feelings/Observations

DAILY JOURNAL
Part 1

Date: **Location:** **Weather:**

DAILY LOG	Cost
Breakfast:	$
Lunch:	$
Dinner:	$
Other:	$
Lodging:	$
Entertainment:	$
Gifts/Souvenirs:	$

Transportation:
    Odometer: _____
    Mi/Km Today: _____
	$

Other:	$

Note Pad		
	Total Today	$
	Total/Trip	$
	Total vs Budget	$

DAILY JOURNAL
Part 2

Location: **Date:**

Experiencing	Comments/Reactions/Feelings/Observations

DAILY JOURNAL
Part 1

Date:　　　　Location:　　　　　　　　　Weather:

DAILY LOG	Cost
Breakfast:	$_____
Lunch:	$_____
Dinner:	$_____
Other:	$_____
Lodging:	$_____
Entertainment:	$_____
Gifts/Souvenirs:	$_____
Transportation: 　　Odometer: _____ 　　Mi/Km Today: _____	$_____
Other:	$_____

Note Pad		
	Total Today	$_____
	Total/Trip	$_____
	Total vs Budget	$_____

DAILY JOURNAL
Part 2

Location: **Date:**

Experiencing	Comments/Reactions/Feelings/Observations

DAILY JOURNAL
Part 1

Date:　　　**Location:**　　　　　　　　**Weather:**

DAILY LOG	Cost
Breakfast:	$_____
Lunch:	$_____
Dinner:	$_____
Other:	$_____
Lodging:	$_____
Entertainment:	$_____
Gifts/Souvenirs:	$_____
Transportation: 　　Odometer: _____ 　　Mi/Km Today: _____	$_____
Other:	$_____

Note Pad		
	Total Today	$_____
	Total/Trip	$_____
	Total vs Budget	$_____

DAILY JOURNAL
Part 2

Location: **Date:**

Experiencing	Comments/Reactions/Feelings/Observations

DAILY JOURNAL
Part 1

Date:	Location:	Weather:	
DAILY LOG			**Cost**
Breakfast:			$_____
Lunch:			$_____
Dinner:			$_____
Other:			$_____
Lodging:			$_____
Entertainment:			$_____
Gifts/Souvenirs:			$_____

Transportation:
    Odometer: _____
    Mi/Km Today: _____
			$_____

Other:			$_____

Note Pad		
	Total Today	$_____
	Total/Trip	$_____
	Total vs Budget	$_____

DAILY JOURNAL
Part 2

Location: _____ **Date:** _____

Experiencing	Comments/Reactions/Feelings/Observations

DAILY JOURNAL
Part 1

Date: Location: Weather:

DAILY LOG	Cost
Breakfast:	$_____
Lunch:	$_____
Dinner:	$_____
Other:	$_____
Lodging:	$_____
Entertainment:	$_____
Gifts/Souvenirs:	$_____

Transportation:
    Odometer: _____
    Mi/Km Today: _____
	$_____

Other:	$_____

Note Pad		
	Total Today	$_____
	Total/Trip	$_____
	Total vs Budget	$_____

DAILY JOURNAL
Part 2

Location: **Date:**

Experiencing	Comments/Reactions/Feelings/Observations

DAILY JOURNAL
Part 1

Date:　　　　Location:　　　　　　　　　Weather:

DAILY LOG	Cost
Breakfast:	$_____
Lunch:	$_____
Dinner:	$_____
Other:	$_____
Lodging:	$_____
Entertainment:	$_____
Gifts/Souvenirs:	$_____
Transportation: 　　Odometer: _____ 　　Mi/Km Today: _____	$_____
Other:	$_____

Note Pad		
	Total Today	$_____
	Total/Trip	$_____
	Total vs Budget	$_____

DAILY JOURNAL
Part 2

Location: **Date:**

Experiencing	Comments/Reactions/Feelings/Observations

DAILY JOURNAL
Part 1

Date: **Location:** **Weather:**

DAILY LOG	Cost
Breakfast:	$
Lunch:	$
Dinner:	$
Other:	$
Lodging:	$
Entertainment:	$
Gifts/Souvenirs:	$
Transportation: 　　Odometer: _____ 　　Mi/Km Today: _____	$
Other:	$

Note Pad		
	Total Today	$
	Total/Trip	$
	Total vs Budget	$

DAILY JOURNAL
Part 2

Location:		Date:
Experiencing	**Comments/Reactions/Feelings/Observations**	

DAILY JOURNAL
Part 1

Date: Location: Weather:

DAILY LOG	Cost
Breakfast:	$
Lunch:	$
Dinner:	$
Other:	$
Lodging:	$
Entertainment:	$
Gifts/Souvenirs:	$

Transportation:
   Odometer: _____
   Mi/Km Today: _____
	$

Other:	$

Note Pad		
	Total Today	$
	Total/Trip	$
	Total vs Budget	$

DAILY JOURNAL
Part 2

Location: **Date:**

Experiencing	Comments/Reactions/Feelings/Observations

DAILY JOURNAL
Part 1

Date: _____ Location: _____ Weather: _____

DAILY LOG	Cost
Breakfast:	$_____
Lunch:	$_____
Dinner:	$_____
Other:	$_____
Lodging:	$_____
Entertainment:	$_____
Gifts/Souvenirs:	$_____
Transportation: 　　Odometer: _____ 　　Mi/Km Today: _____	$_____
Other:	$_____

Note Pad		
	Total Today	$_____
	Total/Trip	$_____
	Total vs Budget	$_____

DAILY JOURNAL
Part 2

Location: **Date:**

Experiencing	Comments/Reactions/Feelings/Observations

DAILY JOURNAL
Part 1

Date:	Location:	Weather:	
DAILY LOG			**Cost**
Breakfast:			$_____
Lunch:			$_____
Dinner:			$_____
Other:			$_____
Lodging:			$_____
Entertainment:			$_____
Gifts/Souvenirs:			$_____
Transportation: Odometer: _____ Mi/Km Today: _____			$_____
Other:			$_____

Note Pad		
	Total Today	$_____
	Total/Trip	$_____
	Total vs Budget	$_____

DAILY JOURNAL
Part 2

Location: _____ **Date:** _____

Experiencing	Comments/Reactions/Feelings/Observations

DAILY JOURNAL
Part 1

Date:	Location:	Weather:	
DAILY LOG			**Cost**
Breakfast:			$_____
Lunch:			$_____
Dinner:			$_____
Other:			$_____
Lodging:			$_____
Entertainment:			$_____
Gifts/Souvenirs:			$_____

Transportation:
    Odometer: _____
    Mi/Km Today: _____
			$_____

Other:			$_____

Note Pad		
	Total Today	$_____
	Total/Trip	$_____
	Total vs Budget	$_____

DAILY JOURNAL
Part 2

Location: **Date:**

Experiencing	Comments/Reactions/Feelings/Observations

DAILY JOURNAL
Part 1

Date: Location: Weather:

DAILY LOG	Cost
Breakfast:	$
Lunch:	$
Dinner:	$
Other:	$
Lodging:	$
Entertainment:	$
Gifts/Souvenirs:	$

Transportation:
    Odometer: _____
    Mi/Km Today: _____
	$

Other:	$

Note Pad		
	Total Today	$
	Total/Trip	$
	Total vs Budget	$

DAILY JOURNAL
Part 2

Location: **Date:**

Experiencing	Comments/Reactions/Feelings/Observations

DAILY JOURNAL
Part 1

Date: Location: Weather:

DAILY LOG	Cost
Breakfast:	$
Lunch:	$
Dinner:	$
Other:	$
Lodging:	$
Entertainment:	$
Gifts/Souvenirs:	$

Transportation:
    Odometer: _____
    Mi/Km Today: _____
	$

Other:	$

Note Pad		
	Total Today	$
	Total/Trip	$
	Total vs Budget	$

DAILY JOURNAL
Part 2

Location: **Date:**

Experiencing	Comments/Reactions/Feelings/Observations

DAILY JOURNAL
Part 1

Date: Location: Weather:

DAILY LOG	Cost
Breakfast:	$
Lunch:	$
Dinner:	$
Other:	$
Lodging:	$
Entertainment:	$
Gifts/Souvenirs:	$

Transportation:
    Odometer: _____
    Mi/Km Today: _____
	$

Other:	$

Note Pad		
	Total Today	$
	Total/Trip	$
	Total vs Budget	$

DAILY JOURNAL
Part 2

Location: _____ **Date:** _____

Experiencing	Comments/Reactions/Feelings/Observations

DAILY JOURNAL
Part 1

Date: Location: Weather:

DAILY LOG	Cost
Breakfast:	$_____
Lunch:	$_____
Dinner:	$_____
Other:	$_____
Lodging:	$_____
Entertainment:	$_____
Gifts/Souvenirs:	$_____

Transportation:
    Odometer: _____
    Mi/Km Today: _____
	$_____

Other:	$_____

Note Pad		
	Total Today	$_____
	Total/Trip	$_____
	Total vs Budget	$_____

DAILY JOURNAL
Part 2

Location: **Date:**

Experiencing	Comments/Reactions/Feelings/Observations

DAILY JOURNAL
Part 1

Date: _____ Location: _____ Weather: _____

DAILY LOG	Cost
Breakfast:	$_____
Lunch:	$_____
Dinner:	$_____
Other:	$_____
Lodging:	$_____
Entertainment:	$_____
Gifts/Souvenirs:	$_____

Transportation:
    Odometer: _____
    Mi/Km Today: _____
	$_____

Other:	$_____

Note Pad		
	Total Today	$_____
	Total/Trip	$_____
	Total vs Budget	$_____

DAILY JOURNAL
Part 2

Location: **Date:**

Experiencing	*Comments/Reactions/Feelings/Observations*

DAILY JOURNAL
Part 1

Date:	Location:	Weather:

DAILY LOG	Cost
Breakfast:	$_____
Lunch:	$_____
Dinner:	$_____
Other:	$_____
Lodging:	$_____
Entertainment:	$_____
Gifts/Souvenirs:	$_____

Transportation:
    Odometer: _____
    Mi/Km Today: _____
	$_____

Other:	$_____

Note Pad		
	Total Today	$_____
	Total/Trip	$_____
	Total vs Budget	$_____

DAILY JOURNAL
Part 2

Location: _____ **Date:** _____

Experiencing	Comments/Reactions/Feelings/Observations

DAILY JOURNAL
Part 1

Date:	Location:	Weather:	
DAILY LOG			**Cost**
Breakfast:			$_____
Lunch:			$_____
Dinner:			$_____
Other:			$_____
Lodging:			$_____
Entertainment:			$_____
Gifts/Souvenirs:			$_____

Transportation:
  Odometer: _____
  Mi/Km Today: _____
			$_____

Other:			$_____

Note Pad		
	Total Today	$_____
	Total/Trip	$_____
	Total vs Budget	$_____

DAILY JOURNAL
Part 2

Location: **Date:**

Experiencing	Comments/Reactions/Feelings/Observations

DAILY JOURNAL
Part 1

Date: **Location:**   **Weather:**

DAILY LOG	Cost
Breakfast:	$
Lunch:	$
Dinner:	$
Other:	$
Lodging:	$
Entertainment:	$
Gifts/Souvenirs:	$

Transportation:
   Odometer: _____
   Mi/Km Today: _____
	$

Other:	$

Note Pad		
	Total Today	$
	Total/Trip	$
	Total vs Budget	$

DAILY JOURNAL
Part 2

Location: **Date:**

Experiencing	*Comments/Reactions/Feelings/Observations*

DAILY JOURNAL
Part 1

Date: Location: Weather:

DAILY LOG	Cost
Breakfast:	$
Lunch:	$
Dinner:	$
Other:	$
Lodging:	$
Entertainment:	$
Gifts/Souvenirs:	$

Transportation:
    Odometer: _____
    Mi/Km Today: _____
	$

Other:	$

Note Pad		
	Total Today	$
	Total/Trip	$
	Total vs Budget	$

DAILY JOURNAL
Part 2

Location: **Date:**

Experiencing	Comments/Reactions/Feelings/Observations

DAILY JOURNAL
Part 1

Date: Location: Weather:

DAILY LOG	Cost
Breakfast:	$
Lunch:	$
Dinner:	$
Other:	$
Lodging:	$
Entertainment:	$
Gifts/Souvenirs:	$

Transportation:
    Odometer: _____
    Mi/Km Today: _____
	$

Other:	$

Note Pad		
	Total Today	$
	Total/Trip	$
	Total vs Budget	$

DAILY JOURNAL
Part 2

Location: **Date:**

Experiencing	Comments/Reactions/Feelings/Observations

AUTOMOBILE
Use

FUEL

Date	Odometer Reading	Gallons/Liters	MPG	Cost Per ( )	Total Cost

OTHER EXPENSES

Date	Odometer Reading	Item	Cost

Notes:

PHOTO Log

Camera Serial No. _____

Roll Number	ASA/ISO	First Shot	Last Shot	Comments
1				
2				
3				
4				
5				
6				
7				
8				
9				
10				
11				
12				
13				
14				
15				
16				
17				
18				
19				
20				

NEW FRIENDS Met

Name & Phone	Address	Comments
☎	✉	
☎	✉	
☎	✉	
☎	✉	
☎	✉	
☎	✉	
☎	✉	
☎	✉	
☎	✉	
☎	✉	

NEW FRIENDS
Met

Name & Phone	Address	Comments
	✉	
☎		
	✉	
☎		
	✉	
☎		
	✉	
☎		
	✉	
☎		
	✉	
☎		
	✉	
☎		
	✉	
☎		
	✉	
☎		
	✉	
☎		

CURRENCY
Exchange

Date	Dollars	Local Currency	Rate	Commission	Net

AFTER Your Trip

Lasting Memories

Top Ten Memories	98
Expense Analysis	99
Next Time	100

Well, your trip is over. All you have left are memories and souvenirs—and a few bills. This last ULTIMATE TRAVEL JOURNAL section will wring out the most from your trip. The charts are best used either on the way home or shortly after you've returned. Grab a comfortable seat, ask your travel partner to join you, and let your mind wander through the best parts of your trip.

TOP TEN
Memories

Page	Description

EXPENSE
Analysis

Per Day Expenses

	Budget Total (p. 7)	*Actual Total*	*Over/ (Under)*
Food: Breakfast	$_____	$_____	$_____
Lunch	$_____	$_____	$_____
Dinner	$_____	$_____	$_____
Other	$_____	$_____	$_____
Lodging:	$_____	$_____	$_____
Entertainment:	$_____	$_____	$_____
Transportation:	$_____	$_____	$_____
Other:	$_____	$_____	$_____
Per Day Totals:	$_____	$_____	$_____

One Time Expenses

Transportation:	$_____	$_____	$_____
Gifts/Souvenirs:	$_____	$_____	$_____
Other:	$_____	$_____	$_____
One Time Totals:	$_____	$_____	$_____

Total Expenses

Grand Totals:	$_____	$_____	$_____

NEXT Time

Now is the best time to start thinking about your next trip. You may have a mild case of the post-trip-blues—or filled with dreams of the future. Either way, you can brighten up your spirits by working out where to go next time. Think about what you liked, didn't like, missed, want to repeat, recommendations from others, etc. Now, write down those things you'd like to do on the next trip. Get a fresh new ULTIMATE TRAVEL JOURNAL and start your planning now!

Ideas for Future Trips

Other Notes:

APPENDICES

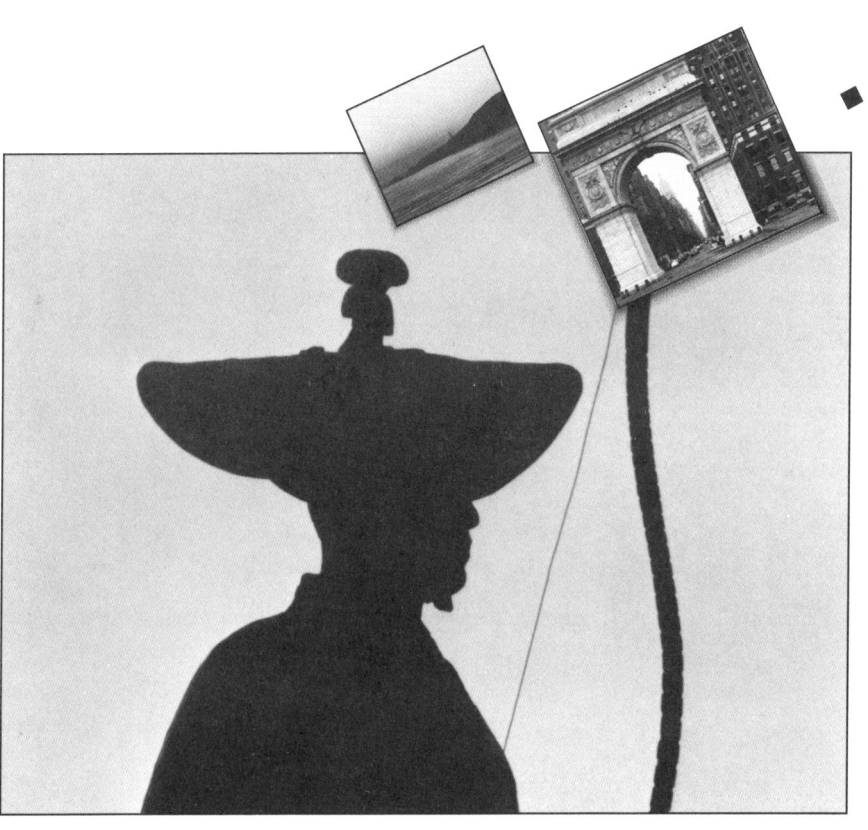

World Map	102-103
Conversions	104-107
Notes & More	108-124

WORLD
Map

WORLD
Map

CONVERSIONS
Time Zones

International Time Zone Conversions
Standard Time—Winter

Time Zones	City, Country
1	Nome, USA
	Pago Pago
2	Anchorage, USA
	Honolulu, USA
	Tahiti
3	Pitcairn Island
4	Los Angeles, USA
	San Francisco, USA
	Vancouver, Canada
5	Denver, USA
	Calgary, Canada
6	Chicago, USA
	Dallas, USA
	Mexico City, Mexico
7	New York, USA
	Washington DC, USA
	Panama City, Panama
	Lima, Peru
8	Bermuda Island
	Caracas, Venezuela
	Santiago, Chile

Time Zones	City, Country
9	Buenos Aires, Argentina
	Rio De Janeiro, Brazil
10	Azores Islands
11	Reykjavik, Iceland
12	London, England
	Madrid, Spain
13	Paris, France
	Rome, Italy
	Berlin, Germany
	Amsterdam, Netherlands
	Lagos, Nigeria
14	Athens, Greece
	Jerusalem, Israel
	Pretoria, S. Africa
	Leningrad, USSR
	Cairo, Egypt
	Beirut, Lebanon
	Istanbul, Turkey
	Helsinki, Finland
15	Moscow, USSR
	Kuwait
	Nairobi, Kenya
	Riyadh, Saudi Arabia
	:30 Tehran, Iran

Time Zones	City, Country
16	Kabul, Afghanistan
17	Karachi, Pakistan
	:30 Delhi, India
	Bombay, India
18	Rangoon, Burma
19	Djakarta, Indonesia
	Bangkok, Thailand
	:30 Singapore
	Kuala Lumpur, Malaysia
20	Hong Kong
	Manila, Philippines
	Beijing, China
	Perth, Australia
21	Tokyo, Japan
	Seoul, S. Korea
	Okinawa Island
22	Melbourne, Australia
	Guam Island
23	Loyalty Island
24	Auckland, New Zealand
	Fiji Island

How to Use: Find your current location in the above chart and determine the time by looking at your watch. Next, find the location whose time you want to know. Now, count the number of "Time Zones" between these two locations and then add or subtract this number from your local time—this will be the time in the required location. Counting in the direciton of lower numbers is time behind your local time and vice versa.

For example: Assume you're in New York at 8:00 AM and you want to know the time in Hong Kong. Counting the "Time Zones" between these two cities yields 11 hours behind or 13 hours ahead—9:00 PM or 21:00. Note that some of the locations are set on the half-hour (e.g. Bombay).

CONVERSIONS
Clothing Sizes

Women	Shoes	US	4	5	6	7	8	9	10
		UK	2	3	4	5	6	7	8
		Europe	35	36	37	38	39	40	41
	Stockings	US/UK	8	8½	9	9½	10	10½	11
		Europe	35	36	37	38	39	40	41
	Blouses Sweaters	US	32	34	36	38	40	42	44
		UK	34	36	38	40	42	44	46
		Europe	40	42	44	46	48	50	52
	Dresses Suits Coats	US	8	10	12	14	16	18	20
		UK	10	12	14	16	18	20	22
		Europe	36	38	40	42	44	46	48
Men	Shoes	US	7½	8½	9½	10½	11½	12½	13½
		UK	6	7	8	9	10	11	12
		Europe	41	42	43	44	45	46	47
	Socks	US/UK	9½	10	10½	11	11½	12	12½
		Europe	39	40	41	42	43	44	45
	Shirts	US/UK	14½	15	15½	16	16½	17	17½
		Europe	37	38	39	41	42	44	45
	Suits & Coats	US/UK	38	40	42	44	46	48	50
		Europe	48	50	52	54	56	58	60

Use the above as a rough guide only—it's always best to try it on before you buy.

CONVERSIONS
Weights & Measures

To Convert From	To	*Multiply By*
miles—mi	kilometers—km	1.61
yards—yd	meters—m	0.91
feet—ft	meters—m	0.30
inches—in	centimeters—cm	2.54
gallons—gal	liters—l	3.79
quarts—qt	liters—l	0.95
pints—pt	liters—l	0.47
ounces—oz	grams—gm	28.35
pounds—lb	kilograms—kilo or kg	0.45
square yards—sq yd	square meters—sq m	0.84
cubic yards—cu yd	cubic meters—cu m	0.77
miles/hour—mph	kilometers/hour—km/hr	1.61
lbs/sq in—psi	kilopascals—kPa	6.89

To convert from Fahrenheit (°F) to Celsius (°C), subtract 32° from °F and then multiply by 5/9.

To convert from Celsius (°C) to Fahrenheit (°F), multiply °C by 9/5 and then add 32°.

CONVERSIONS
Weights & Measures

To Convert From	To	Multiply By
kilometers—km	miles—mi	0.62
meters—m	yards—yd	1.10
meters—m	feet—ft	3.30
centimeters—cm	inches—in	0.39
liters—l	gallons—gal	0.26
liters—l	quarts—qt	1.06
liters—l	pints—pt	2.13
grams—gm	ounces—oz	0.04
kilograms—kilo or kg	pounds—lb	2.20
square meters—sq m	square yards—sq yd	1.19
cubic meters—cu m	cubic yards—cu yd	1.30
kilometers/hour—km/hr	miles/hour—mph	0.62
kilopascals—kPa	lbs/sq in—psi	0.15

When you need a fast estimate and don't have a calculator handy, use the following *approximate* conversions:

1 km = ⁵⁄₈ or 0.6 miles
1 m = 1 yard
1 cm = ¼ inch
1 l = 1 quart
1 kilo = 2 pounds
100 g = 3.5 ounces

100 km/hr = 60 mph
100 °C = 212 °F
21 °C = 70 °F
0 °C = 32 °F

NOTES & More

NOTES & More

NOTES
& More

NOTES & More

NOTES & More

NOTES & More

NOTES & More

NOTES
& More

NOTES & More

NOTES & More

NOTES & More

NOTES & More

NOTES & More

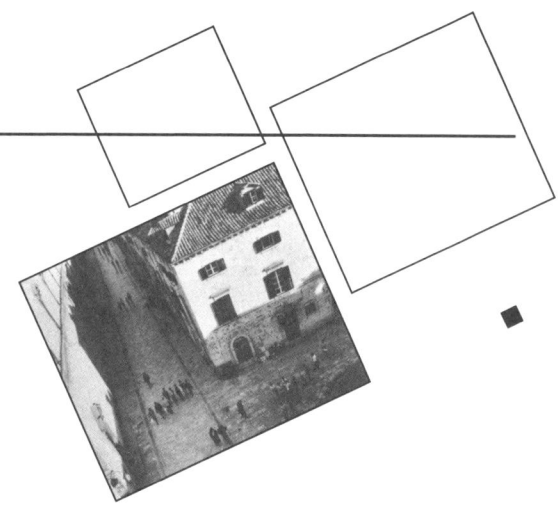

The ULTIMATE TRAVEL JOURNAL is available in three versions:

◆Softcover—Complete and comprehensive with all your favorite sections.

◆Hardcover—Attractive and permanent edition with a special binding allowing the book to lie flat for easier writing.

◆Deluxe Hardcover—The hardcover edition with attractive packaging creating the ideal bon voyage gift.

New copies of any ULTIMATE TRAVEL JOURNAL edition can be purchased directly from The FLORIAN Group. Quantity discounts are also available. For more information contact:

>The FLORIAN Group
>Astoria Building
>P.O. Box 1423
>Lake Oswego, OR 97035

The ULTIMATE TRAVEL JOURNAL is the State-of-the-Art in travel journals and diaries. The FLORIAN Group will continue to develop and publish improvements and new travel products. The best improvements come from users. It is in this spirit that your inputs are solicited. If your idea is used, you'll be notified, recognized, and will receive a free copy of the new edition.

- A Break-through: Innovation in Travel Diaries and Journals

- Easy-to-use: Just Fill in the Blanks Forms, Logs and Records

- Flexibility: A Simple Diary or a Complete Travel Manual

- Top Quality and Appearance: A Cherished and Lasting Gift

- Complete and Thorough: Use Before, During, and After Your Trip.

- A Travel Companion: All the personal information you need in a convenient book that you can carry anywhere.

THE ULTIMATE TRAVEL JOURNAL